Skinny Pigs as Pets

A Complete Owner's Guide

Including Feeding, Caring, Housing, Breeding and Health
Information for Hairless/Bald Guinea Pigs as well as
General Guinea Pig Care Information and Care Sheet

Published by MTH Publishing

ISBN 978-0-9928293-2-2

Cover designed by Dr. Jay Polma
A CIP catalogue record of this book is available from the British Library
Printed and bound in Great Britain
By Lightning Source UK Ltd, Milton Keynes

Disclaimer and Legal Notice

Foreword

In this book you will find a wealth of information about caring for guinea pigs of all types, particularly Skinny Pigs (hairless/bald guinea pigs). Here you will find tips for selecting and raising your Skinny Pigs as well as valuable information on housing, feeding, breeding and health concerns. By the time you finish this book you will be ready to be the best Skinny Pig owner you can be!

Acknowledgements

I would like to extend my sincerest thanks to my family who have always supported my love for my own Skinny Pigs. I could not have done this without you.

Table of Contents

Chapter One: Introduction

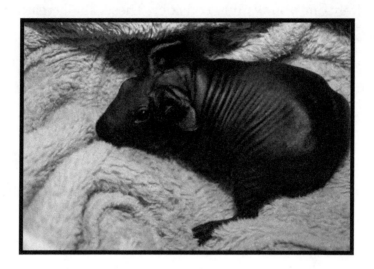

When you think of a guinea pig, you probably picture a large rodent with silky or even spiked hair. You may picture any combination of fur colours from black and white to caramel, brown and cream. What many people do not picture when they think of the words "guinea pig" is a hairless animal with floppy ears and wrinkled skin.

The animal described above is known as the Skinny Pig and it is one of two varieties of nearly hairless (or bald) guinea pigs. The Skinny Pig is hairless on most of its body with the exception of the muzzle, feet and legs. Like regular guinea pigs, Skinny Pigs come in a variety of colours and patterns and they have become quite popular as pets in recent years.

If you are looking for a unique family pet, the Skinny Pig is definitely one you want to consider. These small creatures are very sociable and love to spend time with their owners. Not only are they a very good-natured breed, but they are also highly entertaining, exhibiting a number of unique behaviours and producing a chorus of different noises.

In this book you will learn the basics about Skinny Pigs as well as the information you need to care for them as pets. Much of the information in this book pertains specifically to the care of Skinny Pigs, but most of this information can be applied to the care of other guinea pig breeds as well.

Useful Terms to Know

ACBA – the American Cavy Breeders Association

Alfalfa Hay – a staple in the diet of young guinea pigs; high in protein and calcium

Boar – an intact male guinea pig

Breed – a variant of a particular species; the Skinny Pig is a breed of guinea pig

Cavy – derived from the family *Caviidae,* the family of rodents to which guinea pigs belongs

Herd – a large group of guinea pigs; wild guinea pigs live in herds

Malocclusion – the misalignment of teeth in guinea pigs and other rodents

Nest Box – an enclosed box where a guinea pig can sleep and hide; may be made from a variety of materials

Pellet – a commercial guinea pig food shaped in pellets; typically made from various hays and grasses

Popcorning – a behaviour guinea pigs display when they are happy; jumping straight up and down, often tossing the head and squeaking at the same time

Pup – the term for a baby guinea pig

Rosette – a whorl of hair in a cavy's coat; may appear individually or in clusters

Sow – a female guinea pig

Standard – or Breed Standard, the requirements for showing a particular breed

Sweeps – long locks of hair that fall from a long-haired guinea pigs sides and back

Timothy Hay – a staple in the guinea pig's diet; provides dietary fiber

Wheek – the high-pitched whistle guinea pigs make to call attention to something

Chapter Two: Understanding Skinny Pigs and Guinea Pigs

As it has already been mentioned, the Skinny Pig is a breed of guinea pig – they are unique from regular guinea pigs in that they are nearly hairless. Aside from this and a few other differences, however, the Skinny Pig is just as wonderful a pet as a guinea pig and they are just as easy to care for. Before you decide whether a Skinny Pig is right for you, you would do well to learn everything you can about them. In this chapter you will learn the basics about Skinny Pigs and what makes them different from other guinea pigs. You will also learn some specifics about different types of guinea pigs as well as their history as pets.

1.) *What Are Guinea Pigs?*

The guinea pig is a type of rodent belonging to the family Caviidae in the genus Cavia. The scientific name of the guinea pig is *Cavia porcellus*, which is why they are often referred to as cavies. Though their name might suggest otherwise, the guinea pig is not actually related to pigs nor did they originate in Guinea. Guinea pigs are actually domesticated descendants of large rodents and other cavies native to the Andes Mountains in South America.

Throughout the Western world, guinea pigs have become very popular as pets. Guinea pigs have been present in Western households since the early 16th century and there are currently multiple organisations dedicated to the breeding and showing of these animals. There are many different breeds of guinea pig – some with long hair, others with short hair and some with hardly any hair at all.

Though the details may differ according to breed, guinea pigs typically weigh between 1.5 and 2.5 lbs. (700 to 1200g) at maturity and they measure between 8 and 10 inches (20 to 25 cm) in length. These animals have an average lifespan between 4 and 5 years, though some have been known to live as long as 8 years. In fact, the longest-lived guinea pig is recorded to have lived for almost 15 years.

Guinea pigs are surprisingly intelligent animals – they are able to learn paths to food and remember a certain path for several months. Similar to other rodents, guinea pigs tend to startle easily and they prefer to live in groups (often called "herds"). Guinea pigs are very social and vocal animals – they have very well-developed senses of hearing and touch. The primary means of communication these animals use is vocalisation and some of the most common sounds guinea pigs make include:

Wheeking – a loud, whistle-like noise; a general expression of excitement often made in response to feeding

Purring – a sound made when the guinea pig is happy or enjoying itself; often made in response to petting, grooming or feeding

Rumbling – a low rumbling sound, typically associated with dominance in a group; during courting, a male may rumble and sway while circling the female (sow)

Chutting – sounds made while two guinea pigs are chasing each other

Squealing – a high-pitched sound typically resulting from pain or discontent

Chirping – a sound typically made by baby guinea pigs when they are hungry; likened to a bird song and often related to stress

Chattering – a sound typically made in warning produced by rapidly gnashing the teeth; may be accompanied by a raising of the head

In addition to producing a wide range of sounds, guinea pigs are also loved as pets for their docile temperaments. With frequent handling, guinea pigs can become very tame and amenable to handling. Many guinea pigs tolerate being held for hours and, if properly tamed, most guinea pigs seldom bite or scratch. If given room to roam, however, guinea pigs do like to explore their territory and they will often do so while squeaking or whistling.

Because they are such social animals, guinea pigs should ideally, be kept in pairs or groups. A guinea pig kept entirely on its own is more likely to suffer from stress and/or depression. Keeping multiple male guinea pigs together can be tricky unless they are raised together from a young age. However, there are certain bonding strategies that can be effective in getting a group of guinea pigs to live in harmony if they have not been raised together.

2.) What Are Skinny Pigs?

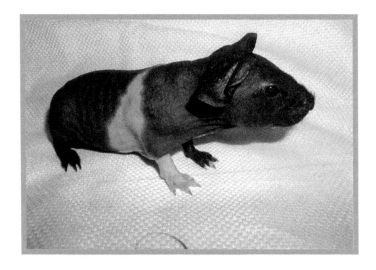

The Skinny Pig is a particular breed of guinea pig and it is almost entirely hairless. These guinea pigs usually have some hair on their muzzles, feet and legs but remain hairless over the rest of their body. Depending on breeding, Skinny Pigs may also exhibit a thin covering of hair on the back as well as the legs. The skin of Skinny Pigs is mostly smooth, though there may be some wrinkling around the legs and neck. The body is full and, despite the name, the spine and ribs should not be visible.

Though they may not have much hair, Skinny Pigs still come in a variety of colours and patterns. Some of the most popular patterns for Skinny Pigs include Dutch, Italian and

Tortoiseshell. Interestingly, the Skinny Pig is not significantly different from the haired guinea pig in terms of physiology. The main difference, of course, is their lack of hair which means that they require more food to maintain their body heat. The ideal temperature for a Skinny Pig is between 75 and 79°F (24 to 26°C).

Because they do not have a protective covering of hair, a Skinny Pig's skin is fairly delicate. The skin has the appearance of human skin, being smooth and supple, but it is no different from haired guinea pig skin. Certain precautions are necessary to protect Skinny Pigs from infection – soft nesting materials are needed to prevent injury and blankets or cloth bags are recommended to aid in body heat conservation.

Some interesting facts about Skinny Pigs include:

- Some Skinny Pigs develop more hair as they age, though they remain mostly hairless

- The metabolism of a Skinny Pig is much higher than that of a haired guinea pig due to the need to maintain body heat without the help of hair

- If you let your Skinny Pig outside during the summer, you may need to use sunscreen to prevent his delicate skin from burning

- Skinny Pigs have many different skin pigmentations including chocolate, cinnamon, albino and Dalmatian

- The Skinny Pig learns quickly and will likely respond with squeaking to the sound of food containers being opened

3.) *Skinny Pigs vs. Regular Guinea Pigs*

As you have already learned, the Skinny Pig is just a specific breed of guinea pig – it still has the same scientific name (*Cavia porcellus*). There are, however, a number of significant differences between the Skinny Pig and some other breeds of guinea pigs. The most obvious difference, of course, is the Skinny Pig's lack of hair. There is a second breed of guinea pig which is known for its hairlessness – the Baldwin guinea pig.

What makes the Baldwin different, however, is the fact that they are born haired but lose their hair between 2 and 5 days after birth. Once they lose their hair, Baldwin guinea pigs are almost entirely hairless except for a little hair on the feet. These guinea pigs are more heavily wrinkled than

Skinny Pigs and they exhibit a variety of colour combinations in skin pigmentation. Another difference between Skinny Pigs and Baldwins is the fact that Baldwins have a rubbery texture to their skin.

Though Skinny Pigs do not vary significantly from haired guinea pigs in terms of physiology, there are some genetic differences. The modern Skinny Pig is the result of a crossing between a haired guinea pig and a hairless laboratory strain of guinea pig. This gene for hairlessness (now referred to as the "Skinny Pig gene" was a spontaneous genetic mutation that was first seen in 1978). The gene for hairlessness is recessive which means that, in order to create a litter of 100% Skinny Pig pups, you need to breed together two full Skinny Pigs.

If you breed a Skinny Pig with a guinea pig that simply carries the Skinny Pig gene, there is a 50% chance of the pups being Skinny Pigs and a 50% chance they will merely be carriers of the gene. Genetics play a very important role in breeding Skinny Pigs (perhaps more-so than with haired guinea pigs) – proper Skinny Pig breeding protocol involves crossing out to a haired carrier at least once every other generation. For this reason, breeding is not recommended for novice Skinny Pig owners.

Summary of Facts

Scientific Name: *Cavia porcellus*

Origins: cross between haired guinea pig and hairless lab strain (a spontaneous mutation)

Weight: 1.5 to 2.5 lbs. (700 to 1200g)

Size: 8 to 10 inches (20 to 25 cm)

Coat: confined to the muzzle, feet and legs

Skin: colour corresponds to variety; somewhat wrinkled

Colour: variety of colours including agouti, self, solid ticked, roan, brindle, tortoiseshell, white, Italian, Dutch and Dalmatian

Lifespan: 4 to 5 years average

Temperament: very social and friendly; can easily be tamed; amenable to handling

Sociability: best kept in pairs or same-sex groups

4.) History of Skinny Pigs as Pets

Contrary to popular belief (based on their name), guinea pigs are neither related to pigs nor are they native to Guinea. In reality, the guinea pig is a type of rodent that was domesticated as early as 5000 BC for use as food by tribes in the Andes Mountains in South America. Archaeological digs have uncovered guinea pig skeletons in Peru and Ecuador dating back to 500 BC and these animals were commonly depicted in ancient Peruvian art created by the Moche people.

During the 16th century, European traders began to bring guinea pigs back to Europe where they quickly established popularity as an exotic pet. Queen Elizabeth I herself is rumoured to have had a guinea pig as a pet. For hundreds of years, the guinea pig was bred and shown in a number of haired varieties. It wasn't until 1978, however, that the Skinny Pig made an appearance.

In 1978, a spontaneous genetic mutation was identified at Montreal's Institute by Armand Frappier – this mutation resulted in hairlessness in a colony of Hartley laboratory guinea pigs. Four years later, in 1982, these guinea pigs were sent to Charles River Laboratories to be bred for use in laboratories and they continue to be popular for use in dermatological studies today. Following their introduction, Skinny Pigs have been out crossed with haired guinea pigs to improve the genetics of the breed.

The first guinea pigs identified with the hairlessness gene were albino. Over time, however, cross-breeding has resulted in the creation of several different colour patterns of Skinny Pigs including broken, rainbow, tortoiseshell and Italian. Though some people believe the myth that Skinny Pigs are weak and sickly, this is most likely the result of inbreeding and improper care. When properly bred and timely crossing with haired guinea pigs, Skinny Pigs can be genetically sound and healthy.

5.) Types of Guinea Pigs

There are many different breeds of guinea pig that have been identified and described, but only 13 have been accepted by the American Cavy Breeders Association (ACBA). The different breeds of guinea pig exhibit not only different coat lengths, but also textures and colours. Below you will find a brief description of each breed of guinea pig divided into categories by coat length/type.

Short-Haired (Smooth-Coated)

There are three "smooth-coated" breed of guinea pigs, named for the fact that their coats are short and smooth. Though their coats may be short, they are still full and consistent in length over the body. These three breeds include the American, American Crested and Ridgeback. Two other breeds, the Rex and Teddy, also have short coats but they are not categorised as "smooth-coated" breeds. Together with the Abyssinian breed, these breeds are categorised as "rough-coated" breeds.

American – this breed is known by several names including the English or simply the Short-Haired guinea pig.

American guinea pigs have consistently short coats with no rosettes.

American Crested – also referred to as the Crested or White-Crested guinea pig, this breed has a short coat with a single rosette on the forehead. In most specimens, the crest is white and white is generally not permitted anywhere else on the body.

1: American Crested Guinea Pig

Ridgeback – this breed of guinea pig is fairly rare, having a short and smooth coat with a ridge running lengthwise down the body. The ridge stands up straight and rosettes may exist on other parts of the body.

Teddy - the Teddy breed has a short and rough coat that is dense and springy in texture, making it stand up all over the body. The length and texture of this breed's coat gives it a soft, toy-like appearance.

2: Teddy Guinea Pig

Rex – this breed is similar in appearance to the Teddy but it has short, rough hair of uniform length no more than ½ inch (1 ¼ cm) all over the body.

Long-Haired

Lunkarya – this breed of guinea pig is often nicknamed Lunk and it was developed in Nordic countries, primarily in Sweden. The Lunkarya has a long, curly coat with a rough texture – it is also very dense and full.

Coronet – this breed of guinea pig resembles the Silkie/Sheltie breed with a long, smooth coat that grows backwards over the body. The main difference is that the Coronet breed has a crest on the forehead.

3: Coronet Guinea Pig

Merino – this breed of guinea pig closely resembles the coronet breed, but it has curly hair.

Alpaca – this rare breed of guinea pig closely resembles the Peruvian breed but it has a curly coat.

Abyssinian – this breed is sometimes classified as a short-haired breed and other times as a long-haired breed. These guinea pigs have rough coats with between 6 and 8 rosettes over the sides, back and shoulders. Ideal specimens of the breed have fully-formed rosettes with tight centers having no hairs sticking out from the middle.

4: Abyssinian Guinea Pig

Peruvian – this breed closely resembles the Silkie/Sheltie breed, having a smooth and long coat. The main difference is that the Peruvian has a prominent forelock growing forward over the face.

Sheba – this breed of guinea pig is also sometimes called the Sheba Mini Yak. These guinea pigs have long, rosetted coats and a generally tousled appearance.

Silkie/Sheltie – this breed has a long, smooth coat that grows backward over the body. This breed has no rosettes and its coat does not have a part – the coat is generally longer in the rear.

5: Silkie/Sheltie Guinea Pig

Texel – this breed has a long coat flowing backward over the body, like a Sheltie's, but it is curly. Most specimens exhibit tightly wound curls, though some are wavier than others. A lengthwise part down the body is acceptable but not preferred.

6: Texel Guinea Pig

Hairless

By now you are already familiar with both hairless breeds of guinea pig, the Skinny Pig and the Baldwin. Both of these breeds require warmer environments and protein-rich foods to maintain their body heat.

Skinny Pig – as it has already been mentioned, the Skinny Pig is a "mostly" hairless breed. Though hairlessness varies from one specimen to another, most Skinny Pigs have only a small amount of hair on the face and feet.

Baldwin – in contrast to the Skinny Pig, Baldwin guinea pigs are described as "nearly" hairless. These guinea pigs are born with a full coat which they shed as they age until they are left with fur only on their feet.

6.) Colours in Skinny Pigs

Guinea pigs come in a wide array of colours and patterns and, though they may not have much hair, Skinny Pigs do as well. Below you will find a list and explanation of some of the most common colours and patterns seen among Skinny Pigs.

Self – the term "self" is used to describe Skinny Pigs having only one uniform colour. There are three different colour categories for self: black, red and white.

Black – as you can imagine, black Skinny Pigs are black with black eyes and black skin. Any hair the Skinny Pig has should be black as well.

Chocolate – a chocolate Skinny Pig has deep brown hair with black skin and eyes. As the Skinny Pig ages, any hair it has may fade in colour to grey or greyish brown.

Tortoiseshell – these Skinny Pigs have patches of red and black colour, often exhibiting a lengthwise seam down the back and belly to divide the colours.

Dalmatian – a Skinny Pig exhibiting this type of colouration is typically white with coloured spots.

Ticked – the term "ticked" describes a colour pattern in the actual hairs of a guinea pig. Rather than being a solid colour, each hair has stripes of two different colours (typically red and black). Depending on breeding, it is possible for a Skinny Pig to have ticked hairs.

Agouti – this is a common colour pattern in guinea pigs, marked by a solid-coloured belly and ticking on the rest of the body.

Chapter Three: What to Know Before You Buy

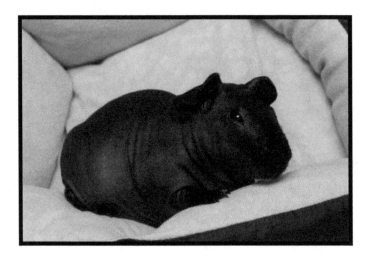

After reading the last chapter, you should have a better idea whether a Skinny Pig or a guinea pig is the right pet for you. Before you actually buy one, however, there are a few more pieces of information you need to consider. For example, do any special licensing requirements apply to this breed in your area? How many Skinny Pigs should you buy and do they get along with other pets? In this chapter you will learn the answers to these questions and more to help you make an educated decision regarding whether the Skinny Pig is the right choice for you.

1.) Do You Need a License?

Before you bring home any kind of new pet, you need to take a moment to research the licensing requirements for your area. Whilst most communities require licensing for dogs and cats, some also have requirements for other pets including small mammals. You do not want to risk bringing home a new pet just to have it confiscated or to be fined for failure to follow regulations. In this section you will learn the basics about licensing requirements for guinea pigs like Skinny Pigs.

a.) Licensing in the U.S.

In the United States, licensing requirements for pets are generally determined at the state level. There are no federal regulations regarding permits or licenses required to keep guinea pigs as pets. The federal government does require guinea pig breeders to follow certain regulations, however. The Animal Welfare Act (AWA), as set forth by the U.S. Department of Agriculture, outlines certain guidelines for individuals who derive over $500 in gross annual income from the sale of guinea pigs.

Though the AWA primarily exists to regulate commercial animal breeding, it can also be used as a guideline for hobby breeders and pet owners. The AWA states that guinea pigs must be housed in an environment that enables it to "make normal postural adjustment with adequate freedom of movement." This act also outlines certain requirements for cage size, temperature, lighting and cage construction.

Even though the U.S. may not require owners of guinea pigs to file for a permit or to obtain a license, you should still follow the basic guidelines set forth by the AWA. It is important to realise that these guidelines describe the absolute minimum level of care required. For example, the AWA states that the cage size for a guinea pig should be 10x10 inches (25x25cm) when most breeders recommend a minimum cage size of 30x36 inches (76x91cm).

b.) Licensing in the U.K.

The U.K. does not have any licensing requirements regarding the keeping or breeding of small animals like the guinea pig. There are, however, strict regulations regarding the import and export of animals. If you are considering bringing a Skinny Pig into the U.K, you may need to apply for an Animal Movement License (AML). These licenses are always required for the movement of livestock but, if you intend to show your Skinny Pigs, you may be legally required to obtain one as well.

As in the United States, pet owners in the U.K. are required to follow the Animal Welfare Act in the care and keeping of their pets. This act was introduced in 2006 and it applies to individual pet owners as well as breeders and farmers. Previous to the passing of this act, action could only be taken once an animal was proven to have suffered. Now, however, the Animal Welfare Act enables enforcement agencies and inspectors to advise and educate pet owners to prevent the suffering of pets like Skinny Pigs from occurring in the first place.

2.) Pet Insurance for Skinny Pigs

When it comes to your own health and the health of your family, you probably have some kind of protection in the form of an insurance policy. What you may not realise, however, is that a similar option is available for your pets. Pet insurance helps owners to mitigate the cost of veterinary services for accidents and illnesses as well as certain preventive care services like spay/neuter surgery.

Not all pet insurance companies offer coverage for Skinny Pigs because they may be considered an "exotic pet." This being the case, you will have to do a little bit of searching around to find a compatible plan. Every plan is different so be sure to compare and contrast covered services as well as premiums and benefits. In many cases, a pet insurance policy works by reimbursing the owner for covered costs so you will need to be sure the service you are getting for your pet is covered before you pay for it.

Pet insurance is not right for everyone, but it is definitely something you want to consider. After all, you never know when your Skinny Pig might become ill and you do not want to have to choose between paying for treatment and losing your beloved pet.

3.) How Many Should You Buy?

As a general rule, you should not keep a single guinea pig by itself – this can result in stress and depression. For the most part, guinea pigs tend to get along best in pairs or trios. You do need to be careful, however, about the make-up of your groups because not all guinea pig will get along together. You need to be especially careful of keeping mixed-sex groups because this could result in unwanted breeding

In most cases, a pair or trio of female Skinny Pigs will get along without any problems. There may be the occasional skirmish or bout of teeth chattering, but you should not have too many problems. Male Skinny Pigs can be a little

trickier, however. If you raise two male Skinny Pigs they may get along or they might eventually have battles over dominance. In some cases, it works best to pair an adult male with a younger male so the older one is undisputed as the boss of the pair. The only way to know for sure how a pair or trio of Skinny Pigs will get along is to try and see how it works out.

4.) Can Skinny Pigs Be Kept with Other Pets?

The answer to this question depends on a number of factors. Some Skinny Pigs are able to get along with other animals while some are not – it largely depends on the temperament of your individual Skinny Pig. One thing you need to consider is the type of pet you are thinking about keeping your Skinny Pig with. Smaller rodents like mice, gerbils and hamsters are not compatible with Skinny Pigs, though a small, gentle rabbit might be. You do have to be careful in keeping different species together to ensure that both animals get the diet they need – if you feed a Skinny Pig rabbit food (or vice versa), he is likely to have some kind of nutritional deficiency.

Outside of keeping your Skinny Pig in the same cage as another pet, the other animals you might be concerned about are cats and dogs. Many Skinny Pig owners have found that their cats get along extremely well with Skinny Pig – you should still supervise all interaction, however, because animals can be unpredictable. Use caution when introducing your Skinny Pig to a dog because you cannot be sure how even the best-behaved dog will react. Dogs tend to have very strong prey drives and you do not want your dog to end up chasing your Skinny Pig around the house.

5.) Ease and Cost of Care

Skinny Pigs not only make wonderful pets, but they are also fairly easy to care for. As long as you provide your Skinny Pigs with adequate shelter, food and attention they should thrive under your care. In this section you will learn not only what kind of things you need in order to care for your new pet, but also what kind of costs you can expect to pay in doing so.

a.) Initial Costs

The initial costs of keeping a Skinny Pig include those costs which are necessary to prepare for and bring your Skinny Pig home. These costs include the purchase price of the animal, the cost of the cage and cage accessories including bedding and food/water dishes. Below you will find an explanation of and an estimate for each cost.

Purchase Price – The cost for a Skinny Pig will vary depending where you buy it – you may pay less at a local pet store, but you cannot be sure that the Skinny Pig you bring home will be healthy. If you want to buy a Skinny Pig of good breeding, you can expect to pay between $75 and $150 (£55.25 to £97.50) for it.

Cage/Habitat – The price you pay for your Skinny Pig's cage will vary depending on its size and the materials from which it is made. You may be able to find a prefabricated cage at your local pet store for $50 (£32.50) or less, but these cages typically do not provide the space that Skinny Pigs need to thrive. Later in this book you will read about C&C cages which are easy to construct and provide plenty of space for Skinny Pigs. Regardless what type of cage you choose, you should plan to spend between $50 and $150 (£32.50 to £97.50) on your Skinny Pig cage.

Cage Accessories – Skinny Pigs are not very needy creatures, so you do not have to worry about spending a lot of money on cage accessories. In addition to providing your Skinny Pig with a food bowl, water dish and hay rack you should also provide some type of shelter. This shelter can be as simple as cardboard box or you can purchase a plastic igloo or some other structure. You should plan to spend between $20 and $40 (£13 to £26) on cage accessories.

Bedding – The bedding you use in your Skinny Pig cage will need to be replaced at least once a week so it is both an initial and a monthly cost. To start your Skinny Pig cage, you should not need to spend more than $10 (£6.50) on bedding.

Tools/Equipment – When it comes to keeping Skinny Pigs, you do not need to invest in a lot of expensive equipment. Skinny Pigs do not have long fur, so you will not need to buy any special brushes. You may, however, want to buy a pair of clippers to keep your Skinny Pig's nails trimmed and you might also want to buy some airtight containers to keep your Skinny Pig's food fresh. The total cost for these items should be under $20 (£13).

Initial Cost Sheet		
Cost Type	**One Skinny Pig**	**Two Skinny Pigs**
Purchase	$75 to $150 (£55.25 to £97.50)	$150 to $300 (£97.50 to £195)
Cage/Habitat	$50 to $150 (£32.50 to £97.50)	$50 to $150 (£32.50 to £97.50)
Accessories	$20 to $40 (£13 to £26)	$20 to $40 (£13 to £26)
Bedding	$10 (£6.50)	$10 (£6.50)
Tools/Equipment	$20 (£13)	$20 (£13)
Total	$175 to $370 (£114 to £240.50)	$250 to $520 (£162.50 to £338)

b.) Monthly Costs

The monthly costs of keeping a Skinny Pig include those costs which are necessary to care for your pet after you bring it home. These costs include the cost of food, bedding, veterinary services and other miscellaneous costs. Below you will find an explanation of and an estimate for each cost.

Food/Treats – The amount of money you spend on food for your Skinny Pigs each month depends on the number of Skinny Pigs you have and the quality of the food you use. Ideally, you should feed your Skinny Pigs a staple diet of high-energy commercial pellets supplemented with plenty of hay and fresh vegetables. Generally, you can expect to spend about $15 (£9.75) per month per Skinny Pig on food.

Bedding – The monthly cost for bedding may vary depending on the size of your cage and the type of bedding you use. For a large cage housing one or two Skinny Pigs, you can expect to pay about $30 (£19.50) per month for wood shavings as bedding. As you will read later in this book, a cheaper alternative to wood shavings is to use fleece as bedding for your Skinny Pigs. This can reduce your monthly bedding costs from $30 (£19.50) to less than $10 (£6.50) per month.

Veterinary Services – Unlike cats and dogs, Skinny Pigs do not require routine vaccinations. You may, however, want to take your pet in for an annual visit to your veterinarian just to make sure he is in good condition. Not all veterinarians are qualified to treat small animals like Skinny Pigs so you may have to pay a little extra to see a specialist. You should expect to pay between $50 and $75 (£32.50 to £55.25) per visit for at least one visit per year. Averaged over 12 months, the monthly cost of veterinary services should be around $6 (£3.90) per month.

Other Costs - In addition to the costs already mentioned, you should factor in unexpected costs into your monthly budget so you are prepared. Some examples of additional costs may include repairs to the cage, replacement of toys or cage accessories and occasional medications (such as for mites). The monthly cost for these items should not exceed $10 (£6.50) and it is not a cost you should expect to pay each and every month.

Monthly Cost Sheet		
Cost Type	**One Skinny Pig**	**Two Skinny Pigs**
Food/Treats	$15 (£9.75)	$30 (£19.50)
Bedding	$10 to $30 (£6.50 to £19.50)	$10 to $30 (£6.50 to £19.50)
Veterinary	$6 (£3.90)	$12 (£7.80)
Other	$10 (£6.50)	$10 (£6.50)
Total	$41 to $61 (£26.65 to £39.65)	$62 to $82 (£40.30 to £53.30)

6.) Advantages and Disadvantages of Skinny Pigs

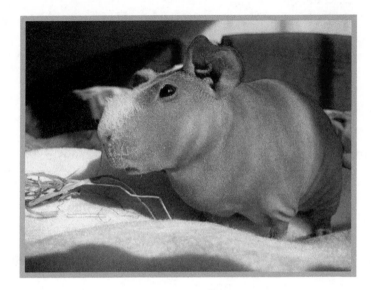

The Skinny Pig is not the perfect pet for everyone, but it may be the right pet for you. Before you buy one, for yourself, take the time to familiarise yourself with the advantages and disadvantages of Skinny Pigs as pets.

Advantages of Skinny Pigs:

- Very friendly temperament
- Gets along very well with children – very gentle
- Very little hair, so shedding is not a key concern

- Generally healthy when given responsible breeding and care
- Love to cuddle with owners and can be tamed
- Very entertaining as pets; interesting behaviour and noises

Disadvantages of Skinny Pigs:

- Eats more food than a haired guinea pig
- Weekly cage cleaning is required
- May require more frequent bathing and skin care than a haired guinea pig
- Cage may take up significant space in the house
- Requires steady supply of fresh hay and produce

Chapter Four: Purchasing Skinny Pigs

If you have decided that a Skinny Pig is the right pet for you, congratulations! You are now ready to move on to thinking about where you are going to buy your new pet. In this chapter you will learn the basics about finding a Skinny Pig breeder and selecting one that is healthy. The last thing you want to do is to bring home your new pet just to find out he is sick. This section will give you all the information you need to know to pick out a Skinny Pig that will give you years of companionship.

1.) *Where to Buy Skinny Pigs*

The Skinny Pig has been growing in popularity of late, regarded as something of an "exotic" pet. This being the case, they are becoming more readily available to the public as pets. If you want to bring home a healthy and happy Skinny Pig, however, you would do well to avoid buying the first one you lay eyes on. It takes time to select a reputable Skinny Pig breeder and to do your research. Though it may mean you have to wait a little longer for your new friend, you will be glad you took the time to make the decision carefully.

a.) Buying in the U.S.

Because they are rising in popularity, you may be able to find Skinny Pigs at your local pet store on occasion. For the most part, however, the market is still higher for haired guinea pigs. This being the case, you may need to step outside the pet store circuit and into the breeder circuit to find a Skinny Pig. Performing a simple online search is one way to find breeders in your area. You can also consult your local pet store or veterinarian for references.

Once you have the information for a few Skinny Pig breeders, you should take your time narrowing them down. Call the breeders and ask for more information about their business and about their experience with the breed. If you are not satisfied that the breeder truly knows what he is doing (and that the Skinny Pig you bring home will be in good condition), move to the next name on your list.

Some questions you might want to ask breeders include:

- How long have you been breeding Skinny Pigs?
- What got you started in the business?
- What is your protocol for maintaining genetic integrity in your breeding lines?
- What do you feed your Skinny Pigs?
- What kind of standards do you implement in regard to your breeding stock?
- How old are your Skinny Pigs when you start/stop breeding them?
- How many times per year do you breed your sows?

If the breeder is able to answer these questions satisfactorily, you can move on to the next stage – visiting the facilities. Depending how far the breeder is from your area, it may not always be practical to make a visit if you do not intend to purchase a Skinny Pig. That is why it is so important to learn everything you can about the breeder before you make your selection.

For Skinny Pig breeders in the U.S, try these links:

World Wide Skinny Pig Association.
<http://www.wwspa.com/skinny-breeders.html>

Margaret's Hairless Guinea Pigs.
http://margaretshairlesspigs.webs.com/aboutourcaviary.html

Hairless Hilltop Hunks.
http://www.hairlesshilltophunks.com/

Bailee's Beauties.
<http://baileesbeauties.weebly.com/the-skinny-breed.html>

b.) Buying in the U.K.

When it comes to purchasing a Skinny Pig in the U.K, your options are very similar to what they are in the U.S. You may be able to find Skinny Pigs at your local pet store, but it will depend on the availability in your area. Even if your local pet store does sell them, you may want to get a little more information before you buy – Who bred the Skinny

Pigs? What is the breeder's experience? Are there any records regarding the health/genetics of the parents?

If you want to buy a Skinny Pig from a reputable source, your best bet may be to find a local breeder. Use the same questions listed above to ascertain the breeder's experience with Skinny Pigs and choose one that seems to have a reputable practice. Another option you might consider in addition to purchasing from a breeder is to adopt a Skinny Pig from a local rescue.

For information on buying or adopting Skinny Pigs, try these links:

Hannah's Skinnies.
http://www.skinnypigsforsale.co.uk/

Piggleswood Skinny Pigs.
http://www.freewebs.com/piggleswoodcavies/

Southern Skinny Pigs.
http://www.southernskinnypigs.co.uk/

2.) How to Select a Healthy Skinny Pig

When you are purchasing a new pet, it is easy to get caught up in the excitement. You may be overwhelmed by the idea that one of those adorable little Skinny Pigs before you will soon be coming home. Do not let your excitement get the best of you. In order to ensure that you bring home the right Skinny Pig, you need to take your time with the decision. In addition to selecting a reputable breeder, you also need to pick the right Skinny Pig from the litter.

Follow these tips for bringing home a healthy Skinny Pig:

- Take the time to make sure the breeder knows what he/she is doing by asking questions.
- Ask for a tour of the facilities – if they are not clean, you should find a new breeder.
- Ask to see the parents of the litter and ascertain their level of health before seeing the pups.
- Check the condition of the cage the pups are kept in – it should be clean with no signs of diarrhoea.
- Observe the pups for a few minutes to see how they interact – they should have no trouble moving and they should be active.

- Check the condition of the pups' skin, eyes, ears and nose – there should be no discharge or discolouration.
- Handle the pups if you can to see how they react to handling – you can also use this opportunity to check their breathing and heart rate.

Once you have determined that the Skinny Pigs themselves are in good condition, you can make your choice. Ideally, you should purchase a Skinny Pig when it is as young as possible – about 6 weeks of age. This gives you the best chance of taming it and building a bond with your new pet while also giving it plenty of time to acclimate to its new life while it is still young.

Chapter Five: Caring for Skinny Pigs and Guinea Pigs

Once you bring your Skinny Pig home, it becomes your responsibility so it is up to you to provide the best care possible. Caring for a Skinny Pig is not significantly different from caring for a guinea pig, but there are a few key differences. In this chapter you will learn the basics about caring for guinea pigs (including Skinny Pigs) in regard to habitat, diet and training. By the time you finish this chapter you will be ready to bring your Skinny Pig home to your family.

1.) Habitat Requirements

The type of habitat you provide for your Skinny Pig is incredibly important because it is where it is going to spend most of its life. Like all guinea pigs, Skinny Pigs are very active and thus require plenty of space in which they can run and play. One thing to be wary of with Skinny Pigs in particular, however, is the sensitivity of their skin – you will need to take a few precautions to keep their skin clean and dry. In this section you will learn everything you need to know about creating the ideal habitat for your precious Skinny Pigs.

a.) Cage Size and Space

Though guinea pigs including Skinny Pigs are the largest type of rodent kept as pets, the cages they are sold in are often not significantly larger than those sold for hamsters and other small rodents. Guinea pigs are very active animals and, as such, they require a great deal of space. For quite some time, the industry standard regarding cage space for a guinea pig was only 2 square feet (per guinea pig). If you take a closer look at a cage this size, however, you will realise that this hardly provides enough space for nesting, feeding and exercise.

<u>More appropriate size guidelines for a guinea pig cage are as follows</u>:

One – 7.5 square feet, or 30"x36" (76x91.4cm)

Two – 10.5 square feet, or 30" by 50" (76x127cm)

Three – 13 square feet, or 30" by 62" (76x158cm)

Four – 13 square feet minimum, ideally 30" by 76" (76x193cm)

If you have ever owned a hamster before, you are probably familiar with the style of cage that includes many tubes and extra levels. These cages are great for hamsters, but they are not ideal for Skinny Pigs because a Skinny Pig needs a large area of open space in which to run around. A large, open cage will give your Skinny Pig room to run and play – it will also minimise territorial issues if you keep several guinea pigs together.

b.) Cage Materials

When it comes to selecting the materials for your Skinny Pig's cage, you need to choose something that will keep it safe. The materials for your cage should be strong enough to keep your Skinny Pig in and other pets out – this also means that the gaps in the wire should be small enough that your Skinny Pig cannot escape through them. The best material for a Skinny Pig cage is coated wire – these materials are strong but will not harm your Skinny Pig if it chews on them.

Try to avoid using a rabbit cage for your Skinny Pig. Rabbit cages are typically designed with slats or wire on the floor but your Skinny Pig requires a solid cage base. Rabbit cages are designed this way to keep the rabbit's feet dry but, as long as you use enough bedding in your Skinny Pig cage, you should not have to worry about this. If you use anything too abrasive on the floor of your Skinny Pig's cage, it could damage your pet's feet and lead to infection.

In addition to the materials from which the cage is built, you also need to think about what type of bedding is best for Skinny Pigs. Regular haired guinea pigs can generally be kept in shaved wood or recycled paper bedding because their fur provides some protection for their delicate skin. This is not the case with Skinny Pigs, however, so you may need to take some precautions.

Some owners have had no problem keeping their Skinny Pig on wood shavings. If you choose this option, however, you should provide a few areas with softer bedding such as a small blanket or a canvas sack where the Skinny Pig can lay down comfortably. As an alternative, you can also consider forgoing wood or paper bedding entirely in favour of fleece.

When using fleece as bedding for your Skinny Pig, you will need to make a few preparations. The fleece will be the top layer of bedding and it will serve to keep your Skinny Pig's feet and skin dry. First, you will need to put down an absorbent layer of towels, paper or some other material. Next, you will need to wash your fleece several times until any waterproof coating has been removed. This way, when your Skinny Pigs relieve themselves in their cage, the water will pass through the fleece and into the absorbent layer, thus keeping its feet dry.

NOTE: Avoid pine and cedar shavings as bedding for your Skinny Pig because these materials contain chemicals that can be dangerous for your pet.

c.) Cage Accessories

As mentioned earlier, your Skinny Pigs needs plenty of space to run and play. This is not to say that you can not include any accessories in your cage, but you should not use any that will obstruct your Skinny Pig's ability to exercise properly. The most important accessories you will need for your cage include: water bottle, food dish, hay rack and hiding places.

Water Bottle – Your Skinny Pig needs constant access to fresh water so it is important that you have a large water bottle in your cage. If you plan to keep more than one Skinny Pig together, you may want to add an extra water bottle. Clean and refill the water bottle daily.

Food Dish – Skinny Pigs tend to perch on their food bowls as they eat, so it is a good idea to buy something that has a wide base – this will keep it from tipping over. The type of material you choose for your bowl is up to you but plastic is a good option because it is inexpensive. Ceramic is also a good option because it is heavy enough that your Skinny Pig is not likely to flip it over and it is easy to clean.

Hay Rack – Hay is an important part of the Skinny Pig's diet so you will need some kind of structure to provide your Skinny Pig with hay. Some owners go with a hay wheel that can be placed anywhere in the cage while others choose a hay rack that is mounted to the cage wall. The goal of a hay rack is to keep the hay clean and dry, up off the floor of the cage.

Hiding Places – Skinny Pigs can be very skittish creatures, so it is a good idea to provide them with a hiding place. Something as simple as a cardboard box can serve well as a hiding place, just be sure it is big enough for your guinea pig. For Skinny Pigs, a hiding place should be lined with some kind of soft bedding to give the animal a comfortable place to lie down.

Other accessories you may choose to give your Skinny Pigs includes treats and toys. A Skinny Pig's teeth grow continuously so you should provide some kind of chew toy to keep them filed down so they do not become maloccluded (misaligned). Wooden chew toys are ideal for this, though cardboard tubes and boxes serve just as well. You can purchase commercial treats for your Skinny Pigs, but you can also save money by using things like dried fruit, pumpkin seeds and bits of fresh fruit.

Unlike a hamster or gerbil, your Skinny Pig does not need a wheel on which to run. In fact, putting your Skinny Pig in a wheel or ball can be very dangerous. Hamsters have flexible spines that allow them to run safely on a wheel – guinea pigs and Skinny Pigs do not, so forcing your Skinny Pig's spine to bend the wrong way could be harmful or even fatal. Your best bet is to simply give your Skinny Pig lots of floor space to run around on for exercise.

d.) Indoor vs. Outdoor

Some guinea pigs can be kept outdoors in a hutch as long as the cage provides adequate protection and the weather does not get too extreme. This is not an option for Skinny Pigs, however, because they are too susceptible to the cold. The ideal temperature range for a Skinny Pig is between 75 and 79°F (24 to 26°C) so, unless you live in a very warm area, your Skinny Pig is unlikely to do well outside.

This is not to say that you cannot give your Skinny Pig some time to exercise outdoors. Having some kind of outdoor pen is a great idea for Skinny Pigs, just be sure there is a lid on the cage so no predators can get into the cage and so your Skinny Pig cannot escape. On sunny days, you may need to protect your Skinny Pig's skin with some sunscreen to keep its skin from burning.

e.) C&C Cages

If you do any research about making your own Skinny Pig cage, you are likely to come across the term "C&C cage". These cages are made using corrugated plastic and metal grids – the name C&C comes from "cubes and coroplast. Coroplast, or corrugated plastic, comes in sheets and can generally be found at your local hardware or home improvement store – this material forms the base of the cage. The walls of a C&C cage are made using the metal grids that are meant to be used to build metal storage cubes – look for these online or at your local Walmart or Target.

To create your own C&C cage, all you have to do is select the proper size using the metal grids and cut the corrugated plastic to size for the base. The metal grids used for the walls of these cages typically measure about 14x14 inches

(36x36 cm) and a cage for a single Skinny Pig should be no smaller than 2x3 grids. For two Skinny Pigs, a cage measuring 2x4 grids is recommended and, for a trio of Skinny Pigs, a cage at least 3x4 or 3x5 grids is ideal.

Once you have selected the size for your cage, connect the proper number of grids using cable ties to create the frame for your cage. Next, measure the corrugated plastic to the dimensions of the cage, adding about 3 to 4 inches on each side. Score one side of the corrugated plastic along the dimensions of the cage and fold up the edges, taping them together at the corners to form the base for your cage. Finally, set the metal grid inside the corrugated plastic base and fill with your preferred bedding.

2.) *Feeding Skinny Pigs*

The diet you offer your guinea pig will play a significant role in determining its overall health and wellbeing. Creating a diet for Skinny Pigs in particular can be a little tricky because their needs are slightly different. In this section you will learn the basics about the nutritional needs of guinea pigs (including Skinny Pigs) as well as some specifics about creating a Skinny Pig diet. You will also receive some tips for offering your guinea pigs fresh vegetables and fruits.

a.) Nutritional Needs

Guinea pigs including Skinny Pigs are herbivorous animals, which mean that they get their nutrition from plant-based sources. Hay is the most important part of a guinea pig's diet and you may offer it in two forms – fresh hay and commercial guinea pig pellets. Most guinea pig owners choose to offer their guinea pigs a combination of fresh hay and pellet foods. This is a good idea for Skinny Pigs as well, but you need to be careful what type of hay and pellets you offer your pet.

When shopping for a commercial pellet for guinea pigs, choose a product that is made from hay, not from corn products or other vegetable fiber. The food should contain at least 8% protein, 16% fiber and at least 1 gram of vitamin C per kg. Unlike many mammals, guinea pigs are unable to synthesise vitamin C so it is something that must come from their diet. If your guinea pig does not get enough vitamin C, it could develop scurvy.

b.) How Much to Feed

It is important to realise that your guinea pig's food has a shelf life – do not purchase a year's worth of food, no matter how tempting that sale price is. Commercial pellet foods are only good for a maximum of one to two months – after this time they will start to lose nutritional value. Over time you will get used to how much your guinea pigs eat and you will learn how to properly stock your food so that it stays fresh.

For young guinea pigs, most guinea pig owners opt for free feeding – that is, leaving the bowl of food full at all times so your guinea pig can graze. For some adult guinea pigs, however, this could lead to overeating. Some guinea pig owners choose to feed their guinea pigs twice a day – two tablespoons of pellets in the morning and two in the evening. It is up to you how you choose to feed your guinea pigs, but keep an eye on its weight and make adjustments as needed if it starts to lose or gain weight.

While you may need to ration your Skinny Pig's consumption of pellet foods, hay should be available at all times. For baby Skinny Pigs, alfalfa hay is recommended because it has the protein and calcium content that growing young guinea pigs need. For adults, however, Timothy or orchard hay are better options because they are higher in dietary fiber.

One important thing you need to realise about Skinny Pigs versus haired guinea pigs is that they require more food to regulate their body temperatures. Because Skinny Pigs do not have hair to keep them warm, their bodies tend to burn fuel faster to produce heat. This being the case, you may need to offer your Skinny Pig more pelleted food than you would a regular haired guinea pig. Again, however, it will take some experimentation on your part to find the right amount for your particular guinea pig.

c.) Fresh Fruits and Vegetables

In addition to plenty of hay and pellets, you should also offer your Skinny Pigs about one cup of fresh vegetables per day and a small serving of fruit once or twice a week as a treat. The best vegetables for Skinny Pigs include leafy greens, fresh herbs, carrots and zucchini. Your Skinny Pigs may also enjoy fruits like apple, orange, banana or berries.

For a longer list of safe fruits and vegetables for your Skinny Pig, see below:

Safe Vegetables

Arugula	Cilantro	Parsley
Asparagus	Cucumber	Parsnips
Beet Greens	Dandelion	Peppers
Broccoli	Greens	Radicchio
Brussels	Endive	Swiss Chard
Sprouts	Kale	Turnip Greens
Cabbage	Kohlrabi	Thyme
Carrots	Lettuce	Zucchini
Celery	Mustard	
Cauliflower	Greens	

Safe Fruits

Apple	Cranberries	Papaya
Banana	Grapes	Pineapple
Blackberries	Honeydew	Plum
Blueberries	Kiwifruit	Strawberries
Cherries	Melon	Watermelon

NOTE: For a complete list, visit
<http://www.happycavy.com/what-can-guinea-pigs-eat/>

d.) Foods to Avoid

Though your Skinny Pigs are likely to nibble on just about anything, there are certain foods that you should avoid. <u>Some foods which could be harmful for your Skinny Pig may include</u>:

Chocolate	Garlic
Potatoes	Mushrooms
Onions	Olives
Caffeine	Rhubarb
Alcohol	Tomato

Chapter Six: Breeding Skinny Pigs

Breeding Skinny Pigs is not something that every owner should endeavour to achieve. Not only do you need to carefully select your breeding stock, but you also have to be careful to breed your Skinny Pigs in the right way and at the right time. If you are thinking about breeding your own Skinny Pigs, read this chapter to determine whether it is really the right choice. If you still feel that it is a good choice for you, continue reading to learn the basics about breeding these wonderful animals and raising the pups.

1.) Basic Breeding Information

Because they only have a lifespan between 4 and 5 years, Skinny Pigs reach sexual maturity fairly early – generally between 4 and 7 months of age for females and around 7 months for males. It is incredibly important to breed female Skinny Pigs at the right time because attempting to breed it too early or waiting too long could be dangerous. Before they reach one year of age, the pelvic bones of the female will fuse which, unless she has already birthed a litter, could make breeding very dangerous.

A female Skinny Pig is capable of conception as early as 2 months of age but, for her own safety, she should not be bred until at least 4 months of age. Male Skinny Pigs, on the other hand, mature between 6 and 8 months so you should wait until at least 7 months old to breed. Breeding a male guinea pig too early could result in a weak litter.

Another challenging aspect of breeding Skinny Pigs is the genetics involved. As you already know, hairless Skinny Pigs are the result of a spontaneous genetic mutation. Only two full Skinny Pigs can be mated to produce a full Skinny Pig litter – if one is only a carrier, the percentage of hairless Skinny Pig pups may be reduced by half. Before you breed your Skinny Pigs, it is essential that you know whether they are both full Skinny Pigs.

Because it takes two full Skinny Pigs to produce a litter of hairless Skinny Pigs, the gene pool for the breed is more limited than it is for haired guinea pigs. This being the case, it is recommended that sows be bred out to a haired carrier at least once every other generation. Not all of the pups resulting from this mating will be hairless Skinny Pigs, but it will help to strengthen the genetic pool.

2.) The Breeding Process

The estrus cycle for a female Skinny Pig lasts between 15 and 17 days, though she may only be receptive to a boar for 8 to 10 hours during this cycle. There are a few signs you can look for to tell when a sow is in season. One tell-tale sign is that the female will begin curving her spine downward in order to elevate her rear end. The female may also begin to mount other females in the same cage. If you are planning to breed your Skinny Pigs, you will need to learn the signs of estrus so you can introduce the male and female at the right time.

Once you introduce the boar and the sow, it should not take long for the mating process to begin – the male will be very eager to breed. It is important to realise that conception may not occur after just one breeding. In fact, you may need to keep the pair together for several days or until you are sure the female is pregnant. Once conception occurs, the female will go through a gestation period lasting between 59 and 73 days (about 9 to 11 weeks).

The average litter of Skinny Pig pups is 3 to 4, though a sow is capable of carrying between 1 and 7 pups in a single litter. As the female progresses in her pregnancy, it will start to develop a distinct pear shape and its weight will increase steadily – it may even double by the end of the pregnancy. During pregnancy, it is important to feed your sow a high-quality diet with a little extra protein and vitamin C. It may also begin to drink more water than usual.

3.) Raising the Babies

Your pregnant Skinny Pig may or may not build a nest before going into labour, but it is wise to provide a nesting box. This is especially important for Skinny Pigs because the pups will need to be kept warm after they are born. For guinea pigs, labour is usually fairly short, lasting only 15 to 45 minutes from the start to the birth of the first pup. You should not see any blood before the pups are born – if you do, contact a veterinarian immediately.

During the birthing process, the sow will hunch its back during each contraction. It will reach under her own belly to pull the pup out and then progress to cleaning it. In most cases, the female has time to clean each pup after giving birth but it is possible for the pups to come too quickly. If the sow gives birth to another pup before cleaning the last one, you may have to step in and do it yourself. Use a clean towel and, very gently, remove the sack and dry it off.

At birth, baby Skinny Pigs typically weigh between 70 and 100 grams. Unlike many mammals, Skinny Pig pups are born fully developed and ready to walk. Depending on the size of the litter, the pups may even begin to sample pellet food after just a few days and most will be weaned between 10 and 14 days after birth. Once the babies have been weaned, it is essential that you separate the pups from the mother. A female Skinny Pig can go into heat very soon after delivery, so you want to avoid getting it pregnant again too soon.

Because female Skinny Pigs become sexually mature as early as 4 months old, you must separate the sexes before that happens. It can be very difficult to tell the sex of baby Skinny Pigs for sure, so you will need to check on them as they grow. In raising your baby Skinny Pigs, make sure they have plenty of fresh water at all times and access to as much hay and commercial pellet food as they like. You do not have to limit the amount of food the guinea pigs get until they are at least 6 months old.

Chapter Seven: Keeping Skinny Pigs Healthy

Your Skinny Pig is more than just a pet – he is your friend and companion. This being the case, you should want to do everything in your power to keep your new friend happy and healthy. Skinny Pigs, like all guinea pigs, are prone to developing certain health problems so you should do your best to learn about these problems before you bring your new pet home. The more equipped you are with valuable knowledge, the better you will be able to handle any problems that arise. In this chapter you will learn about the common health conditions affecting the breed as well as some tips for preventing illness.

1.) Common Health Problems

Regardless of how well you take care of your Skinny Pig, it is likely to become sick at some point. You should not consider this a failure on your part – it is simply a part of life. You may not have complete control over whether or not your pet gets sick, but you can certainly control how you handle the situation. The more you know about illnesses that could potentially affect your Skinny Pig, the better equipped you will be to handle them. The speed with which you react to your Skinny Pig's illness will play a key role in its recovery.

Some of the most common conditions affecting Skinny Pigs include:

- Bumblefoot
- Dental Problems
- Diarrhoea
- Mange Mites
- Respiratory Infection
- Ringworm
- Vitamin C Deficiency (Scurvy)

In the following pages you will find an explanation of each

of these conditions including symptoms, causes and treatment options. By learning about these conditions ahead of time, you will be able to give your Skinny Pig the treatment it needs to make a full recovery.

Bumblefoot

Also known as ulcerative pododermatitis, bumblefoot is a fairly common problem in captive Skinny Pigs. This condition typically results from the Skinny Pig being kept on a hard, abrasive surface or from wire mesh floors. Bumblefoot occurs when the footpads become swollen and ulcerated, creating pressure sores which can be incredibly painful for the Skinny Pig. If not treated, the infection can spread to the bone or tissue and cause permanent damage.

The most effective prevention for bumblefoot is to keep Skinny Pigs on a soft floor with plenty of bedding to prevent damage to the footpads. Unfortunately, this condition can be very difficult to treat and severe cases may result in amputation. The first step is to diagnose the condition as early as possible by culturing the bacteria to find the right antibiotic to use. Treatment with antibiotics accompanied by daily foot soaks may be necessary for at least 4 months as well as topical antibiotics for any open sores or wounds.

Dental Problems

Because a Skinny Pig's teeth grow continuously, dental problems are fairly common. One of the most common dental problems seen in Skinny Pigs is malocclusion – or overgrowth in the teeth. Some common symptoms of this condition including drooling, weight loss and difficulty eating. If the condition gets too bad, the Skinny Pig could actually end up starving in the presence of plenty of food. You should check your Skinny Pig's teeth regularly to make sure they are not overgrown and provide plenty of chew toys to help keep them worn down.

Diarrhoea

Like rabbits, Skinny Pigs possess a fairly sensitive gastrointestinal tract which makes them particularly prone to diarrhoea. Mild cases of diarrhoea may be the result of feeding too much fruit or it could be the result of a change in the Skinny Pig's diet. In severe cases, however, it is often the result of bacterial overgrowth in the intestines, damaged intestinal tissue or some kind of infection. Infections that are likely to cause diarrhoea include bacterial infections and parasites like coccidian and cryptosporidia.

In addition to the diarrhoea itself, some common symptoms of gastrointestinal upset include loss of appetite, dehydration, low body temperature and lethargy. If your Skinny Pig is exhibiting signs of diarrhoea, it is essential that you get it to a vet as soon as possible. Your vet will likely perform a faecal culture to identify the problem then treat with medications such as antibiotics.

Mange Mites

You may be inclined to think that mites and other parasites only affect haired guinea pigs, but Skinny Pigs are just as much at-risk. The most common signs of mange mites are scaly skin, open sores and excessive scratching. Mange mites is actually a parasitic infection and it can be extremely dangerous – even fatal – if not treated properly. The most common treatment for this condition is a topical Ivermectin application administered 7 to 10 days apart. In most cases this treatment, combined with responsible husbandry and adequate sanitation, is adequate to eradicate the infection.

Respiratory Infection

One of the most common respiratory infections seen in Skinny Pigs is pneumonia. This disease can be incredibly dangerous, so you need to treat it as soon as possible. Pneumonia in Skinny Pigs may be caused by a number of different bacteria including *Streptococcus* and *Bordetella.* Your Skinny Pigs may even harbor these bacteria without showing any symptoms but, if the animal becomes stressed or if the environment is not kept clean, they can succumb to infection.

Pneumonia can spread quickly, so if one of your Skinny Pigs falls ill you must separate it immediately. The bacteria responsible for this infection can be spread through direct contact, airborne contact or contaminated food or cage objects. Some initial symptoms of the disease may include discharge from the nose and eyes, sneezing, difficulty breathing and loss of appetite. Once the bacteria has been identified, the infection can typically be treated with antibiotics.

Ringworm

Young Skinny Pigs are especially prone to developing ringworm, particularly in crowded environments.

Ringworm is not actually a worm but a fungal infection that tends to develop in animals that are stressed by poor nutrition and sanitation. Even healthy Skinny Pigs can be carriers of the disease but they may not succumb until they become stressed or their health is otherwise compromised.

Ringworm infections typically manifest in the form of round, crusty scabs. These lesions tend to occur most frequently around the face and ears, but they can spread to the legs and back. Once your veterinarian makes a diagnosis of the problem, your Skinny Pig will likely be treated with a topical antifungal medication. You should also be sure to keep your Skinny Pigs cage clean – during treatment and afterward to prevent a recurrence.

Vitamin C Deficiency

Scurvy, or vitamin C deficiency, is especially common in Skinny Pigs because they are not able to synthesise this nutrient like some mammals can. This being the case, vitamin C is considered an "essential" nutrient which must be present in the Skinny Pig's diet. Vitamin C can come from fresh food sources like broccoli, bell peppers, strawberries and cauliflower – it is also a common additive in commercial guinea pig pellets.

The recommended daily dose of vitamin C for Skinny Pigs is between 10 and 50 mg. Unfortunately, vitamin C breaks down very quickly so adding a supplement to the water may not be effective in cases of deficiency. This is also why it is important to use Skinny Pig foods within 90 days. Some symptoms of vitamin C deficiency include swollen joints, diarrhoea, slow healing of wounds, skin problems and a lack of appetite.

2.) Preventing Illness

When it comes to preventing illness in your Skinny Pigs, there are several things you can do. The most important thing you must do, however, is to provide a high-quality and healthy diet. Do not be tempted to purchase commercial foods for your Skinny Pigs that are full of "treats" like nut and seeds – your Skinny Pig does not actually need these food and they could contribute to obesity. Look for a commercial pellet made from Timothy hay that contains at least 8% protein and 16% fiber.

In addition to a healthy diet, you should also make sure your Skinny Pigs get plenty of exercise. Having a large enough cage that provides plenty of floor space is great, but you should also give your Skinny Pigs time to run around on the floor or in a pen. You can also let your Skinny Pigs run around outside as long as you keep them contained and protect them from overheating.

Another aspect of Skinny Pig care that is unique to this particular breed is regular bathing. A Skinny Pig's skin should be soft and pliant, not rough or scaly. If your Skinny Pig's diet is inadequate or if you do not bathe it properly, it could develop dry, itchy skin and it might be more prone to infection. Bathe your Skinny Pig every two to four weeks with a very mild shampoo to prevent fungal infections and to keep its skin in good health.

Unlike dogs and cats, Skinny Pigs do not require regular vaccinations. In fact, you may not even need to take your Skinny Pig to the vet very often unless there is a problem. Keep in mind that not all veterinarians are qualified to care for Skinny Pigs so you should do some research and have the information for a qualified vet in hand in case you need it. It is always better to be safe than sorry.

Chapter Eight: Showing Skinny Pigs

Skinny Pigs are not only an excellent choice as a pet, but they also make great animals for show, particularly for children. If you are thinking about showing your Skinny Pigs, take the time to learn everything you can about the process before you start it for yourself. You will need to familiarise yourself with the Skinny Pig breed standard to ensure that your pet meet the criteria. You should also learn a bit about how a Skinny Pig show works so you can fully prepare yourself. If you truly want to show your Skinny Pig, this is one chapter you will not want to miss.

1.) Breed Standard

Before you can show your Skinny Pig, you need to make sure that it meets the standards for the breed. The American Cavy Breeders Association (ACBA) and the British Cavy Council are some of the main organisations responsible for drafting and publishing the Standards of Perfection for each breed. The ACBA has not yet accepted the Skinny Pig for show, but various specialty clubs hold their own shows for the breed. The following breed standard for Skinny Pigs is provided by the UK Skinny and Baldwin Cavy Club:

Breakdown of Points (Total = 100 points)

Condition (Show Presentation and Body) – 20 points

Conformation (Head, Ears, Eyes, Body) – 20 points

Colour – 10 points

Coat – 20 Points

Degree of Hairlessness – 30 points

2.) *What to Know Before Showing*

In addition to knowing the breakdown of points for the Skinny Pig breed, you should also understand how points are assigned in each category. Below you will find an explanation of each section of the Skinny Pig breed standard so you can determine how well your own Skinny Pig meets the requirements for show:

Condition

The Skinny Pig should be in good health and fit. The ideal weight range is between 800 and 1200 grams or about 1.5 to 2.5 lbs.

Conformation

The skin should be clean and firm as well as being warm to the touch. The belly may be prominent but the animal should not be overweight. Skinny pigs should have bold, bright eyes and ears that rise slightly from the base and then droop. The overall body shape should be compact with strong shoulders.

Colour

Multiple colours and patterns are acceptable but the colour should be determined from the hair on the Skinny Pig's face and feet – skin colour should correspond to hair colour. In self-coloured specimens, the colour should be even over the entire body. Agouti and ticked specimens should show ticking on the face and feet – only agouti specimens should have a distinctive belly band. Distinctive patterns should be visible in tortoiseshell specimens and markings should be well defined in Dutch and Dalmatian patterns.

Coat

The coat should be confined to the face (primarily on the nose and across the ears) as well as the feet. The fur should be kinked and wiry in texture.

Faults and Disqualifications

- Visible scars, scratches or wounds on the body
- Hair extending beyond the face and feet
- Skin colour not corresponding to hair colour
- Any visible skin defects

Chapter Nine: Skinny Pigs Care Sheet

Throughout this book you have received valuable information about caring for guinea pigs in general as well as specific information about Skinny Pigs. There may come a time, however, when you need to reference a specific fact but do not want to flip through the entire book. That is where this care sheet comes into play – you can quickly reference all of the most relevant facts about Skinny Pigs within the next few pages. Save yourself the time of skimming through an entire chapter and use these quick-reference guides about general Skinny Pig information as well as tips for housing, feeding and breeding.

1.) Basic Information

Scientific Name: *Cavia porcellus*

Origins: cross between haired guinea pig and hairless lab strain (a spontaneous mutation)

Weight: 1.5 to 2.5 lbs. (700 to 1200g)

Sise: 8 to 10 inches (20 to 25 cm)

Coat: confined to the muzzle, feet and legs

Skin: colour corresponds to variety; somewhat wrinkled

Colour: variety of colours including agouti, self, solid ticked, roan, brindle, tortoiseshell, white, Italian, Dutch and Dalmatian

Lifespan: 4 to 5 years average

Temperament: very social and friendly; can easily be tamed; amenable to handling

Sociability: best kept in pairs or same-sex groups

2.) Habitat Set-up Guide

Size Requirements (one): 7.5 square feet, or 30"x36" (76x91.4cm)

Size Requirements (two): 10.5 square feet, or 30" by 50" (76x127cm)

Size Requirements (three): 13 square feet, or 30" by 62" (76x158cm)

Space Needs: plenty of open floor space for exercise

Cage Accessories: water bottle, food bowl, hay rack, hiding places, chew toys

Cage Materials: coated wire, solid bottom

Bedding: shaved wood (not pine or cedar), recycled paper, fleece

Temperature Range: 75 and 79°F (24 to 26°C)

Indoor vs. Outdoor: cannot be kept outdoors

3.) Nutrition Needs/Feeding Guide

Type of Diet: herbivore

Staple Foods: hay and commercial pellets

Pellet Food: look for 8% protein, 16% fiber, 1g vitamin C per kg

Feeding Frequency: free feeding for pups, twice per day for adults

Amount to Feed (adult): 2 tablespoons twice per day (adjust as needed)

Type of Hay: alfalfa for pups, timothy for adults

Tips: feed Skinny Pigs more than haired guinea pigs to support higher metabolism

Preferred Vegetables: lettuce, fresh herbs, carrots, kale, spinach, kohlrabi, cabbage, broccoli, endive

Preferred Fruits: apple, banana, berries, melon, kiwi

Foods to Avoid: chocolate, potatoes, onion, garlic, mushrooms, rhubarb, tomato, caffeine/alcohol

4.) Breeding Tips

Sexual Maturity (female): average 4 to 6 months

Sexual Maturity (male): average 6 to 8 months

Estrus Cycle: 15 to 17 days

Gestation Period: 59 to 73 days

Litter Size: 1 to 7, average 3 or 4

Birth Weight: 70 to 100 grams

Weaning Age: 10 to 14 days, depending on birth weight

Chapter Ten: Frequently Asked Questions

Even after reading this book, you may still have some questions about the care and keeping of Skinny Pigs. In this chapter you will find some of the most frequently asked questions about guinea pigs, Skinny Pig and their care in the following categories:

General Care
Housing
Feeding
Breeding
Health Concerns

General Questions

Q: *Do I need to bathe my Skinny Pig?*

A: Because Skinny Pigs do not have hair, their skin is very fragile and sensitive. This being the case, you need to do a little more work to keep it clean and healthy than you would with a haired guinea pig. You should bathe your Skinny Pig every 2 to 4 weeks with a very mild shampoo. After bathing, pat your Skinny Pig's skin dry – do not rub it and never use a hairdryer.

Q: *How can I keep my Skinny Pig's teeth from becoming overgrown?*

A: A Skinny Pig's teeth grow constantly, so you need to provide them with things to chew on to keep them filed down. Hard chew toys made of wood or cardboard are good options and they are also easy to come by.

Q: *How often do I need to clean my Skinny Pig's cage?*

A: The answer to this question depends on the number of Skinny Pigs you keep and the type of bedding you use. If you use fleece bedding, you may need to vacuum up droplets every other day and wash/replace the fleece once a week. If you use traditional wood or paper bedding, you can simply refresh the bedding every few days (if needed) and replace it entirely once a week. The more Skinny Pigs you have in a cage, the more often you are going to need to clean it out.

Q: *What is the proper way to hold my Skinny Pig?*
A: Always be careful when picking your Skinny Pig up and be sure to support his stomach and back legs with one hand. To make your Skinny Pig feel more secure, hold it against your chest or on your lap.

Q: Why is my Skinny Pig jumping around and squealing?
A: This behaviour is referred to as "popcorning" and it is a guinea pig's expression of joy. Skinny Pigs popcorn in different ways, but many jump straight up into the air on all fours – some even toss their heads and let out a high-pitched squeal.

Housing Questions

Q: *Where should I keep my Skinny Pig's cage?*
A: There are several things to consider when choosing a location for your Skinny Pig's cage. You want to choose an area where your Skinny Pigs will get plenty of attention and human interaction, but they should not be constantly underfoot. Look for an area where your Skinny Pigs will stay warm, but keep them away from direct sunlight or heating vents. Make sure your Skinny Pig's cage is away from drafts and not next to anything that will be very loud (such as a TV or radio).

Q: *Why can Skinny Pigs not be kept outdoors?*
A: Haired guinea pigs can withstand a temperature range between 65 and 75°F (18 to 24°C) because they have the protection of their fur. Skinny Pigs, however, have no fur to help retain their body heat so they must be kept in a temperature range between 75 and 79°F (24 to 26°C).

Q: *What are the benefits of fleece bedding?*
A: Fleece bedding is an excellent choice for Skinny Pigs because it is gentle on their skin. This type of bedding also

makes less mess than wood shavings and helps to keep your Skinny Pigs' feet and skin dry. Using fleece bedding can also save you money because you can simply wash the fleece rather than buying a whole new bag of bedding each time you clean the cage.

Feeding Questions

Q: *What treats can I offer my Skinny Pigs?*
A: While you can find Skinny Pig "treats" at the pet store, these may not be the healthiest options. Try offering your Skinny Pigs cilantro, red bell pepper, dried fruit or nuts and seeds as occasional treats.

Q: *Why is alfalfa hay only recommended for babies?*
A: Alfalfa hay is very high in protein and calcium, two nutrients which are essential for supporting the growth of baby Skinny Pigs (pups). In adults, however, fiber is more important which is why it is best to switch to a high-fiber hay like Timothy hay in adulthood.

Q: *When can I expect my baby Skinny Pigs to start eating pellets?*

A: Unlike some mammals, Skinny Pig pups are fully developed at birth – this means that while they may continue to nurse from their mothers, they are capable of eating and digesting pellet food at a very early age. Skinny Pig pups can be fully weaned between 7 and 14 days, depending on their size at birth.

Breeding Questions

Q: *How can I be sure all my pups will be Skinny Pigs?*
A: The only way to achieve a 100% Skinny Pig litter is to breed two true Skinny Pigs together. If you breed a Skinny Pig with a Skinny Pig gene carrier, you will only have a 50% to 75% chance of Skinny Pig babies.

Q: *When can I start breeding my Skinny Pigs?*
A: Skinny Pig sows can safely be bred starting around 4 months of age. If you wait until the Skinny Pigs reaches 1 year of age (12 months), the bones in its pelvis may have already fused which could make birthing more difficult and dangerous for the Skinny Pig. Male Skinny Pigs (boars) can be bred as early as 7 months of age.

Q: How many pups should I expect from a litter?

A: Skinny Pigs typically give birth to between 1 and 7 pups in a single litter, the average being 3 to 4.

Q: *Why are my two male guinea pigs suddenly fighting?*

A: If you purchase two young guinea pigs together, they will likely get along just fine until they approach sexual maturity. At this point, the battle for dominance begins. In many cases, your guinea pigs will not seriously injure each other but they will keep fighting until one establishes his dominance over the other.

Q: *Why should not I breed my Skinny Pigs?*

A: You should never breed your pets if the only reason for doing so is to make a profit. Breeding Skinny Pigs in particular, has added challenges due to genetic complications. Due to the genetics of this breed, Skinny Pigs must be crossed out to haired guinea pigs every other generation – if you are inexperienced with the breed and fail to do this, your Skinny Pig pups could be small and unhealthy.

Health Concerns

Q: *Can guinea pigs get scurvy?*

A: You may be surprised to learn that scurvy is actually fairly common in guinea pigs. If your guinea pigs do not get enough vitamin C in their diet, they could develop this disease. Prevent this problem from affecting your guinea pigs by offering them plenty of hay and fresh vegetables.

Q: *Are Skinny Pigs more prone to skin problems?*

A: As long as you provide adequate care for your Skinny Pig, it should not have any more skin problems than a regular hair guinea pig. Keep in mind, however, that your Skinny Pig will be more prone to draughts and irritants from harsh bedding.

Q: Does the hairless gene affect the Skinny Pig's health?

A: It is a common myth that Skinny Pigs are "weak" or "sickly" compared to haired guinea pigs. While some Skinny Pigs may be weak or sickly, it is likely due to improper breeding and lack of genetic variety – not simply due to the fact that they possess the gene for hairlessness. If properly cared for, Skinny Pigs can be just as healthy as regular haired guinea pigs.

Q: *Are Skinny Pigs susceptible to ringworm?*

A: Because they do not have hair to protect their delicate skin, Skinny Pigs may be more susceptible to certain fungal infections like ringworm than other haired guinea pigs. Ringworm typically produces patches of red, dry skin and it is particularly common in humid environments.

Q: *Should I be worried if my Skinny Pig gets diarrhoea?*

A: Mild diarrhoea could be the result of too many fresh fruits or a change in your Skinny Pig's diet. If your Skinny Pig develops severe diarrhoea, however, it could be a cause for concern. Severe diarrhoea could be a symptom of infection, so take your Skinny Pig to the vet for a diagnosis and for advice on treatment.

Chapter Eleven: Relevant Websites

In reading this book, you have received valuable information about the care and keeping of guinea pigs in general, as well as specific information about the Skinny Pig. Here you have found tip and facts about housing, raising, feeding and breeding these wonderful animals but you may still want to know more. If you are looking for more information about Skinny Pigs, this is the right place to turn. In this chapter you will find an assortment of relevant websites regarding food, care, health concerns and show information for Skinny Pigs as well as general guinea pig information.

1.) *Food for Skinny Pigs*

In this section you will find relevant websites for information regarding the feeding of Skinny Pigs.

United States Links:

"Skinny Pig." Animal-World. http://animal-world.com/encyclo/critters/guin_pig/SkinnyPig.php

"Feeding." The Urban Pocket Pig. http://www.skinnyguinea.us/feeding.html

"What Can Guinea Pigs Eat? – The Guinea Pig Safe Food List." Happy Cavy. http://www.happycavy.com/what-can-guinea-pigs-eat/

"Vegetables and Fruit." Jackie's Guinea Pigs. http://www.jackiesguineapiggies.com/fruitandveg.html

United Kingdom Links:

"Feeding Guinea Pigs." Galen's Garden.
http://www.guinea-pig-information.co.uk/feeding-guinea-pigs/?doing_wp_cron=1395096041.2053349018096923828125

"Guinea Pig Diet." RDSA.org.uk.
http://www.pdsa.org.uk/pet-health-advice/guinea-pigs/diet

"The Guinea Pig Food and Feeding Guide." Kornage.co.uk.
http://www.kornage.co.uk/feeding_guinea_pigs.html

2.) Care for Skinny Pigs

In this section you will find relevant websites for information regarding the care of Skinny Pigs.

United States Links:

"Care." Bailee's Beauties.
http://baileesbeauties.weebly.com/care.html

"Hairless Guinea Pig – The Skinny Pig." Pet Circle.
http://www.petcircle.com.sg/hairless-guinea-pig-the-skinny-pig/

"Hairless Guinea Pig Care." Margaret's Hairless Guinea Pigs.
http://margaretshairlesspigs.webs.com/hairlessguineapigcare.htm

United Kingdom Links:

"How to Look After a Hairless Guinea Pig (Skinny Pig)." Pets4Homes. http://www.pets4homes.co.uk/pet-advice/how-to-look-after-a-hairless-guinea-pig-skinny-pig.html

"Skinny Pigs." Rodents with Attitude.

http://www.rodentswithattitude.co.uk/skinnypigs.html

"Caring for a Skinny Pig." SkinnyPigsNW.

http://skinnypigsnw.co.uk/care-sheet---the-basics.php

3.) Health Info for Skinny Pigs

In this section you will find relevant websites for information regarding the health of Skinny Pigs.

United States Links:

"Emergency Medical Guide." Guinea Lynx. http://www.guinealynx.info/emergencymedicalguide.html

"Guinea Pigs – Problems." VCA Animal Hospitals. http://www.vcahospitals.com/main/pet-health-information/article/animal-health/guinea-pigs-problems/1070

"Guinea Pig Health." Guinea Pig Manual. http://www.guineapigmanual.com/guinea-pig-health/

Pavia, Audrey. "Common Guinea Pig Health Issues." Small Animal Channel. http://www.smallanimalchannel.com/guinea-pigs/guinea-pig-health/common-guinea-pig-health-issues.aspx

United Kingdom Links:

"Guinea Pig Health and Welfare." RSPCA.org.uk.
http://www.rspca.org.uk/allaboutanimals/pets/rodents/guineapigs/health

"Looking After Your Guinea Pig." Blue Cross for Pets.
http://www.bluecross.org.uk/2152-2805/caring-for-your-guinea-pig.html

"Guinea Pig Health." PDSA.org.uk.
http://www.pdsa.org.uk/pet-health-advice/guinea-pigs

"Guinea Pig Health." Guinea-Pig-Information.co.uk.
http://www.guinea-pig-information.co.uk/guinea-pig-health

4.) General Info for Guinea Pigs

In this section you will find relevant websites for general information regarding guinea pigs as pets.

United States Links:

"Communication." The Urban Pocket Pig.
http://www.skinnyguinea.us/behavior.html

"Tips for Keeping Guinea Pigs Happy and Healthy." The Ann Arbor News. < http://www.annarbor.com/pets/ask-the-veterinarian-guinea-pig-guide/>

"Guinea Pigs: Breeds and Colours." Drs. Foster and Smith.
http://www.drsfostersmith.com/pic/article.cfm?articleid=2586

United Kingdom Links:

"Guinea Pigs." RSPCAorg.uk.
http://www.rspca.org.uk/allaboutanimals/pets/rodents/guineapigs

"A Suitable Environment for Guinea Pigs." RSPCA.org.uk.
http://www.rspca.org.uk/allaboutanimals/pets/rodents/guin
eapigs/environment

"Why Keep Guinea Pigs." Southern Cavy Club.
http://southerncavyclub.co.uk/guidancewelfare/why-keep-
guinea-pigs/

5.) *Showing Skinny Pigs*

In this section you will find relevant websites for information regarding the showing of Skinny Pigs.

United States Links:

"Skinny Pig Breed Standard of Perfection." Cavalier Cavies. http://www.cavaliercavies.com/?page_id=3041

"Your Guinea Pig: A Kid's Guide to Raising and Showing." Wanda L. Curran. http://www.amazon.com/Your-Guinea-Pig-Raising-Showing/dp/0882668897

"Introducing the Show Cavy." http://www.home.netspeed.com.au/reguli/showcavy.htm

United Kingdom Links:

"A Brief Guide to Showing Guinea Pigs (Cavies)." British Cavy Council. http://www.britishcavycouncil.org.uk/Novice/Showing/nov-showing-intro.shtml

"Transporting Your Cavy to the Show." British Cavy Council. http://www.britishcavycouncil.org.uk/ Novice/Showing/nov-showing-procedure.shtml

National Cavy Club. http://www.nationalcavyclub.co.uk/

Index

A

B

C

D

E

F

G

H

I

L

M

N

V

W

Photo Credits

6 By created by Gerbil's daughter (created by Gerbils daughter) [GFDL (http://www.gnu.org/copyleft/fdl.html) or CC-BY-SA-3.0 (http://creativecommons.org/licenses/by-sa/3.0/)], via Wikimedia Commons, <http://commons.wikimedia.org/wiki/File:Guinea_pig-Meerschweinchen.jpg>

7 By Kazulanth at en.wikipedia [Public domain], from Wikimedia Commons, <http://commons.wikimedia.org/wiki/File:Guinea_pig_you ng.jpg>

Agouti By 4028mdk09 via Wikimedia Commons, <http://en.wikipedia.org/wiki/File:D%C3%B6sendes_Haus meerschweinchen.JPG>

Silkie By Christine via Wikimedia Commons, <http://en.wikipedia.org/wiki/File:Peruvian_cavy.jpg>

Crested By Brent Moore via Wikimedia Commons, <http://commons.wikimedia.org/wiki/File:2006_TN_State_F air-_Guinea_Pig.jpg>

Texel By Just chaos (calexpo 346) [CC-BY-2.0 (http://creativecommons.org/licenses/by/2.0)], via Wikimedia Commons,

<http://commons.wikimedia.org/wiki/File:Texel_guinea_pig .jpg>

Coronet By Abrahami via Wikimedia Commons, <http://en.wikipedia.org/wiki/File:Coronet_cavia.JPG>

Abyssinian By Tavu via Wikimedia Commons, <http://en.wikipedia.org/wiki/File:AniarasKelpoKalle.jpg>

Teddy by Pixabay User Jolly_Sunshine, <http://pixabay.com/en/guinea-pig-josie-pet-young-fluffy-233121/>

References

Birmelin, Immanuel. *Guinea Pigs: A Complete Pet Owner's Manual*. Barron's Educational Series, Inc.: New York. 2008.

Curran, Wanda L. *Your Guinea Pig – A Kid's Guide to Raising and Showing*. Storey Communications, Inc.: Pownal, Vermont. 1995.

"Emergency Medical Guide." Guinea Lynx.
<http://www.guinealynx.info/emergencymedicalguide.html>

"Guinea Pig Feeding." The Humane Society of the United States.
<http://www.humanesociety.org/animals/guinea_pigs/tips/guinea_pig_feeding.html>

"Guinea Pig Glossary." The Wheekly Reader.
<https://wheeklyreader.wordpress.com/tag/guinea-pig-terminology/>

"Guinea Pig Glossary of Terms." Drs. Foster and Smith.
<http://www.drsfostersmith.com/pic/article.cfm?aid=2519>

"History of the Baldwin Guinea Pig." Baldwin Guinea Pigs.
<http://baldwinguineapigs.weebly.com/history.html>

"How to Look After a Hairless Guinea Pig (Skinny Pig." Pets4Homes. <http://www.pets4homes.co.uk/pet-advice/how-to-look-after-a-hairless-guinea-pig-skinny-pig.html>

Mancini, Julie. *Guinea Pigs*. Animal Planet. TFH Publications: New York. 2006.

Pavia, Audrey. *Your Happy Healthy Pet Guinea Pig (2nd Edition)*. Wiley Publishing, Inc.: Hoboken, New Jersey. 2005.

"Piggy Care FAQ." Hairless Guinea Pig Sales. <http://hairlessguineasales.weebly.com/skinny-faq--care.html>

"Skinny Pig Breed Standard of Perfection." Cavalier Cavies of Michigan. <http://www.cavaliercavies.com/?page_id=3041>

"Skinny Pig Origin." Margaret's Hairless Guinea Pigs. <http://margaretshairlesspigs.webs.com/skinnypigorigin.htm>

"Skinny Pigs." Rodents with Attitude. <http://www.rodentswithattitude.co.uk/skinnypigs.html>

Somerville, Barabara and Bucsis, Gerry. *Training Your Pet Guinea Pig*. Barron's Educational Series, Inc.: Hauppauge, New York. 2012.

"USDA Regulations on Environment." Guinea Pig Cages. <http://www.guineapigcages.com/USDA.htm>

"What Are Common Health Problems in Pet Guinea Pigs?" RSPCA.org.au. <http://kb.rspca.org.au/What-are-the-common-health-problems-in-pet-guinea-pigs_294.html>

"What Can Guinea Pigs Eat? – The Guinea Pig Safe Food List." Happy Cavy. < http://www.happycavy.com/what-can-guinea-pigs-eat/>

"When Breeding Skinny Pigs." Margaret's Hairless Guinea Pigs. <http://margaretshairlesspigs.webs.com/skinnypigbreeding.htm>

CPSIA information can be obtained
at www.ICGtesting.com
Printed in the USA
BVHW010636210120
569936BV00010B/10